THE LIBRARY
VICTORIA

·33134 (41) Maed.

A WINDOW ON
THE WORKPLACE?

Pupils' and Employers' Views
of a Work Experience Scheme

C MacDonald
H D Black

EDINBURGH UNIVERSITY LIBRARY
WITHDRAWN

The Scottish Council for Research in Education

This is one of a series of reports prepared by the Scottish Council for Research in Education's evaluation team for the *Transition to Adult Life Project* of the Glasgow Division of Strathclyde Regional Council. The project is sponsored by the European Community's *Transition of Young People from Education to Adult and Working Life* programme and Urban Aid.

The SCRE evaluation team for this project comprises:
H D Black, Senior Research Officer
C MacDonald, Research Officer

For further information on the TAL project contact:
Mrs E Lennie
TAL Project Co-ordinator
Glenwood Secondary School
147 Castlemilk Drive
GLASGOW G45

For further information on the TALP Evaluation (or about SCRE's evaluation service in general) contact:
H D Black
Senior Research Officer
SCRE
15 St John Street
EDINBURGH EH8 8JR

Cover based on a design by Eugene Gallacher.

ISBN 0 947833 18 8

Published 1987.

©1986   The Scottish Council for Research in Education. All rights reserved. No part of this publication may be reproduced or transmitted in any form or by any means, electronic or mechanical, including photocopy, recording, or any information storage and retrieval system, without permission in writing from the publisher.

Printed and bound in Scotland for The Scottish Council for Research in Education, 15 St John Street, Edinburgh EH8 8JR, by D & J Croal Ltd, Haddington.

CONTENTS

Foreword

Schemes in which pupils are given the opportunity to obtain a 'taste' of the world of work through short-term placements in a work environment are increasingly seen as valuable additions to the school curriculum. Common sense seems to tell us that these 'work experience' programmes must be of benefit to youngsters who are shortly to leave school. But, surprisingly, relatively little research has been undertaken to assess the effects of work experience and to see whether it is in fact serving a useful purpose.

One of the ways in which the *Castlemilk Transition to Adult Life Project* has been trying to widen the educational environment of pupils has been to offer work experience. This booklet provides an account of the operation of this scheme in one school and tries to assess its effects on the pupils. It also presents the views of that often forgotten partner in work experience programmes — the work providers. An account of the ways in which project staff have sought to develop the approach is set out in the preface by the Project Co-ordinator. The project participants and evaluators hope that by making their experience available, other schools who are considering implementing similar schemes may learn something about the potential effects and limitations.

The researchers wish to record their appreciation of the cooperation and goodwill they received from a number of sources. The organisations which provided placements for pupils gave us a great deal of their time, despite heavy work schedules. The youngsters involved in the project willingly answered our questions and often talked at length and with great insight into their experiences. And their teachers gave us valuable support in arranging for writing exercises to be carried out and in organising interviews.

The Co-ordinator of the *Castlemilk Transition to Adult Life Projects* Evelyn Lennie, and the teacher responsible for organising the work experience programme in School B both provided considerable support during the planning of this study and were always available for consultation.

This evaluation study is funded as part of the European Community's Action Programme on the Transition of Young People from Education to Adult and Working Life Project and further supported by an Urban Aid Grant. We gratefully acknowledge the financial assistance which Glasgow Division of Strathclyde Regional Council has given us.

Preface

Evelyn Lennie, the Project Co-ordinator, gives an account of work experience within the Castlemilk Transition to Adult Life Project —

The *Castlemilk Transition to Adult Life Project* is the Scottish part of a network of 30 Projects set up by the European Community throughout ten of the member countries with the common theme of transition from education to adult and working life. The Castlemilk Project, which involves the three area secondary schools, aims to increase the ability of schools to prepare young people for life and work, to improve industry's understanding of the aims and methods of schools, and to develop closer links between the project schools and their local communities.

To help pupils make the transition from school, we make use of the services of adults other than teachers and utilise the out-of-school environment as a learning resource; we include work experience, community service and attendance at a local further education college; we lay emphasis on familiarisation with new technology and on the provision of vocational guidance. This report examines the work experience scheme as it is organised in one of the three schools involved in the project. This school was chosen as the focus of the study because it offered work experience to the greatest number of pupils — all youngsters in the final year of compulsory schooling (S4) were offered the opportunity to go out on placements, although this was optional and not compulsory.

We believe it is important for young people to have the chance to sample adult working life, not primarily from a vocational point of view, because a week is not long enough for them to absorb many new skills, but as part of the young person's maturing process. They see for themselves what adult working life is like, experience the discipline of work, the need to work to a standard within a particular time; they learn to work in a team with adults and to cope with longer hours and more travelling. They gain a broader view of work, having experience of a job which may not be their future career choice. They discover factors about themselves which will influence their job choice. They may find they enjoy dealing with the public or doing routine work but on the other hand they may find they dislike working outside or working in a noisy environment. It is very important that these findings are discussed during debriefing sessions. We hope they have a successful experience so that they gain in self confidence and realise that they can cope with work. The pupils are also keen to obtain a good testimonial which they can use as a reference for a first job.

In the school chosen for this study, work experience has been offered for several years both to non-certificate pupils throughout the school session and to certificate pupils in the month of June. Since the aims of the scheme were being achieved and the worth of the scheme could be seen, the school staff agreed that all pupils in S4 should be offered the chance of a week's work experience in the month of October, half the group going out one week and the rest the following. For students who are under the age of fifteen, community placements are arranged. School staff find they can use this time profitably with the opportunity of working with smaller classes. The teacher responsible for the organisation of the scheme spends a great deal of time contacting existing and new employer participants in the scheme, preparing pupils for placements, visiting them during their week's work experience and debriefing them on their return to school.

We are very grateful to all the companies and organisations who take our pupils on placements. Through the links we have established with them further developments have been possible. Discussions with employers have influenced the content of the Work Preparation Course, mock interviews with pupils either in school or in their companies' premises have been arranged. In addition to the work experience offered in S4, students in S5 have been given the chance of workshadowing. The aim of this is vocational as it allows students to observe people working in jobs or professions which they are considering as their career choice and which require further training.

In the Castlemilk Transition Project we are preparing young people for adult life. We have found that despite the high level of unemployment the young people still aim to begin their adult life as young workers. With the help of the employers who participate in the work experience scheme we are endeavouring to improve their chances of getting and keeping a job.

1
INTRODUCTION

What is work experience?

Work experience is a rather nebulous term: it can refer to a variety of experiences with diverse and often undefined objectives. It also describes an experience that is qualitatively different from being in full-time employment. As Watts (1983) pointed out:

> It refers not to the full experience of work, but to something *less* than this experience. To be precise, the term is applied to schemes in which people experience work tasks in work environments but without taking on the full identity of a worker.

Work experience in schools has been criticised on a number of grounds but primarily as being unrepresentative of the realities of work: the youngsters are only in the workplace for a short time and have none of the pressures arising from the routineness of work and the need to perform adequately. However, despite the inadequacies inherent in the approach, work experience is still advocated as one of the most suitable methods for providing pupils with an opportunity to see what is involved in a particular job, for introducing them to social and work practices and for giving youngsters the chance to engage in relationships with adults outside the traditional pupil-teacher relationship. So even if work experience cannot provide students with a completely realistic picture of the workplace, it is still seen as serving the useful purpose of removing some of the mystique about the world of work, and thus contributing to the preparation of youngsters for their transition from school to adult life.

However, relatively little research has been undertaken to assess the effects of work experience and to see whether it is serving a useful purpose. Watts, in his review of the existing literature, found the available evidence was reasonably positive, but noted that most of the writing in this field had concentrated on *how* to undertake such schemes rather than *why* to.

Our study, therefore, was undertaken in order to look at the operation of a work experience scheme in one school and to evaluate its effects on the pupils. Since we felt also that, in the past, the views of one of the important partners in such schemes — the work providers — had been overlooked, their reactions to the work experience programme were also investigated.

1

The school's work experience programme

Because of time pressures, we decided to look at the operation of the work experience scheme in only one of the three schools involved in the Castlemilk Transition to Adult Life Project. School B was chosen because it offered work experience to the greatest number of pupils: *all* youngsters in the final year of compulsory education (S4) were offered the opportunity to go out on placements although this was optional and not compulsory. In the event 86 of the 130 pupils took up this option.

For administrative reasons, placements were arranged in two blocks in October 1985; 42 pupils went out in Block 1 and 44 in Block 2. Some of the younger students who were not within twelve months of the minimum school leaving age were ineligible (under the 1973 Education Act) for employer-based schemes and instead were offered placements in community organisations. One teacher, Ms B, was primarily responsible for the organisation of the scheme: she contacted new employers, maintained contact with existing participants and allocated placements. She was also responsible for visiting pupils during their week's work experience.

The research study

We interviewed 18 pupils and 18 employers about their views of work experience. Although certain lines of enquiry were pursued (for details see Appendices I and II) these interviews were not too formally structured since we wanted to provide the degree of flexibility necessary for the emergence of issues which were important to the interviewees. Additional information was obtained from a larger sample of pupils who were given writing tasks, and by inspecting pupils' reports written after the work experience and pupil log books kept during placements. (More information on these are given in Appendix III).

This report is divided into three sections. The first section presents the employers' views. Section 2 — the pupils' views — is divided into two parts. The first part is concerned with pupils' perceptions of and reactions to the scheme as this emerged from the interviews. The second provides a brief summary of what they saw, both before and after their placements, as the useful aspects of work experience. This is based on information gathered from the pupils' writing.

Finally, in Section 3, we draw together the views of both the employers and the pupils, and discuss the value of the scheme.

2

EMPLOYERS' VIEWS OF WORK EXPERIENCE

Although the success of a work experience scheme depends to a large extent on the organisations in which pupils are placed, little is known about how these 'work providers' feel. Why do they take part in such schemes? Are there any benefits to them from the scheme or is participation simply an altruistic act? What do they think of the pupils? And what do they see the value of such a programme being to the youngsters?

It was important to try to find out the answers to these questions for three reasons — to see how well the school's and providers' expectations matched (differences might suggest areas in which communication could be improved) — to investigate whether work experience served purposes other than those traditionally expected — to examine whether there were any benefits to the employers, since, if there were, this could be used to encourage other organisations to take part.

This section begins by looking at employers' reasons for participating in the work experience scheme and their opinions as to the benefits for both themselves and for industry in general. It then describes the types of activity in which pupils were involved, the training and supervision available and the advice given on recruitment and job applications. It looks at employers' views on the value of work experience to the pupils and at the impressions that employers had of the pupils. Finally, the role of the school in the scheme and employers' satisfaction with the work experience programme in general are considered.

The employer study

Throughout this report the terms 'employers' and 'industry' are used to describe, respectively, the providers of placements and the organisations in which students were based. Thus 'employer' can refer to the manager of a firm, a personnel manager, a member of staff in the workplace — whichever representative of the firm we interviewed. Similarly, 'industry' or 'the workplace' can refer to a construction firm, a hairdresser, a library, a school etc — whichever organisation pupils were placed in.

In the scheme operated by the school there were 22 different *work-based* organisations in which pupils could be placed. The placements offered, each lasting one week, covered garage work, the construction industry, the retail trade, a hotel (offering kitchen and dining room duties, chambermaid duties and portering), a factory, hairdressing, veterinary practices, libraries, clerical work and a hospital (including portering, catering, domestic work and clerical work). We interviewed 16 of these work-based employers and made sure that our sample represented all of the types of work available.

The 8 *community* organisations offered work in old peoples' homes, primary schools, a charity (offering clerical work), a centre for the handicapped and community centres. Only two community based employers were interviewed (from the charity and a primary school) but these two organisations provided places for half of the pupils allocated to community placements.

The following table shows the total number of employers involved in the scheme, the number of pupils who had placements in these organisations in Blocks 1 and 2, and our interview sample. The sample of employers covered organisations which provided placements for around 70% of the pupils.

Organisations	*Work-based*	*Community-based*	*Total*
Total number	22	8	30
Number of pupils on such placements	58	28	86
Employers interviewed	16 (covering 17 placement organisations)	2	18 (covering 19 placement organisations)
Number and percentage of pupils in the sample organisations	46 (79%)	14 (50%)	60 (70%)

Table: The Employer Sample

Just under half (8) of the employers in the sample said that they had been providing placements for pupils from this school for one year or less and a further 8 for less than three years. Only two had said that they had been participating in the School's work experience scheme for three years or more. Eight of the employers offered work experience to youngsters from the case study School only (although two had previously taken pupils from other schools). Seven were involved with one other school and only three offered placements to two or more schools.

Employers' reasons for participation

Employers may take part in a work experience scheme for many different reasons. Some may see it as a social service, while others may feel that more tangible benefits will accrue for themselves. Because the question of reasons for participation was potentially sensitive, we decided to tackle the issue in a number of different ways during the course of the interview. We began by asking interviewees why they had decided to become involved in the scheme and, later, questioned them about whether their organisation gained anything from participation. We also included a question on the related issue of whether industry in general benefited from pupil placements.

Most of the organisations in the work experience programme had been contacted by the teacher responsible for placements asking if they would be willing to take part. Three of the participants, however, had become involved in other ways. One, a garage owner who was involved in youth work, had been approached by a teacher at the school who was both a customer and a member of the same youth organisation; the second was an organisation whose chairman had visited the school and had offered to help in any way he could; and the third was a contact made through Project Trident.[1]

Social obligation

Most of the participants said that they were pleased to take part either because it seemed to be a worthwhile project or because they were conscious of their social obligation to help youngsters.

"I thought the principle of work experience was useful. For several years we've been involved with other schools . . . It's a good scheme, especially for those not academically orientated."

"I've a great belief in doing what we can to help young people — in giving them an insight into what working life is like . . . We thought if we could help in any way then we'd like to."

Many of the interviewees spoke of the value of the programme being that pupils could gain an insight into a work environment and into a specific trade or job before they left school. They felt that they were providing a service to pupils in that they were giving them a chance to see what work was like and whether they would like that particular job.

"We've a responsibility, if this is the way education is going, to provide work experience because of unemployment and because pupils aren't getting, through

---

[1] Project Trident is a national initiative which aims to help pupils to discover their potential abilities through undertaking challenging pursuits, voluntary work and work experience.

5

their families, a realistic outlook on jobs. Being a local employer, we have an obligation to let people in and, if it's realistically practical, to actively participate in this kind of scheme."

"It's all about getting pupils to be prepared to work rather than preparation for work."

"It lets the young people see how things are in hairdressing as opposed to how they think it is."

Several of the employers had decided to become involved with this school in particular because they had a link with Castlemilk.

"We [the owners] are both Castlemilk boys — so that's why we got involved. Coming from there, we felt for the kids. It sounds corny but it's true."

"I used to go to [the school] . . . so I thought 'Well, give them a hand'."

"We recruit from Castlemilk. It seems only fair that since we recruit from that area that, when asked, we should be willing to take part in work experience."

Direct benefits to their own organisation

When asked about the benefits of the scheme to their own organisation just under half said that they did not gain anything themselves but were instead fulfilling a social obligation to help youngsters. However, other employers saw practical benefits for themselves. Three said that they gained an "extra pair of hands", although one qualified this by saying that the benefit was only marginal because quite a lot of staff time was taken up with showing pupils what to do and in supervising them. A further three interviewees stated that they benefited from having an open-ended lookout for potential employees.

"It gives me a chance to find out more about them and the way they work than you could do at an interview. You learn more about their capability and potential."

A few of the employers saw participation in the programme as a good public relations exercise.

"I don't really know if we gain terribly much from it but I don't think it does us any harm. And it can only do us good in the eyes of the community."

One of the libraries thought that the publicity they got from the scheme might encourage youngsters to feel "more friendly" towards the library and so more likely to use its facilities.

A fair number of the interviewees saw the placements as a way of keeping in touch with what pupils felt and finding out more about the needs and outlook of young people.

"It makes us try to adapt our thoughts to providing for youngsters who are coming out of school and who are facing unemployment . . . We've been used to fourth and fifth years who're doing Highers and who are probably going to enter college . . . So this type of work experience helps us to learn to deal with and talk to other types of youngsters."

It was also thought that the youngsters provided a stimulus in the work environment by allowing the full-time workers to see their workplace "through new eyes".

"The things we're asking pupils to do is sort of highlighting areas of our business that need looking at. So if you're doing something like this well, you can turn back something you're giving and doing for these young people to your own advantage."

". . . it's good for [the workers] to have someone fresh and innocent at their elbow asking questions because it sharpens them up. You're asked a question, 'Why do you do this?', and you've done it for years and you ask yourself 'Well, why do I do that, is there a better way?'."

A small number of employers also saw benefits for themselves in terms of staff co-operation and an opportunity to learn more about other employees.

"By introducing the young person into the firm and saying 'Here's someone, we can do something', it builds team work in here. It's fantastic just how much interest everyone takes, how they co-operate."

"We also learn a lot about our own employees. If you just see someone all day bashing nails into a piece of wood and then one day you take a young person along, you can see this worker's attitude . . . this person maybe feels part of the scene more than they did before because he had been asked to tell the youngster something."

One interviewee felt that the work experience scheme helped with staff training. Because this particular store did not have a very large staff turnover, young supervisors did not get as wide a training as they might. The work experience programme, therefore:

"....is good for the supervisors because it's taking them through the training procedure. When we have these pupils in, it's keeping the procedures fresh in the supervisor's mind, in identifying training needs with a newcomer . . . They're having to use appraisal techniques constantly in this one week, whereas with the more experienced sales staff, they don't really have to use it to the same degree."

Benefits to industry in general

Two of the employers did not know what the benefits of the programme were to industry in general and a further three felt that there were really only benefits for the pupils themselves. The others, however, thought that industry did gain from what the pupils learned during their placements. The youngsters learned about the realities of working life and were able to try out skills and interests before committing themselves. This was seen as benefiting industry because it meant that new recruits coming to them had a broader experience and were therefore more likely to have realistic expectations of work and perhaps be better able to make career choices.

"If you have kids who have a wee bit more experience and who have been in different working environments it broadens a pupil's experience. You bring your past experience to your new job, which can only help an employer."

The work experience scheme was also seen as industry's opportunity to contribute to education.

"The whole point of education, to my mind, is really for discovering one's talents and, hopefully, allowing you to use it to the best of one's ability. But industry can't get back out of education what they don't put into it. This way everyone's getting the chance to tell young people 'the facts of life'."

Other interviewees saw the benefits as being more practical. The programme provided both an extra pair of hands and a platform for recruitment. One of the employers felt that work experience provided industry with a better basis for selecting recruits because pupils came to interviews with more experience. This made a recruitment officer's job easier since it presented a topic around which discussion could take place.

"It also makes the youngsters a wee bit more interesting, the fact that they have something to talk about at interviews. Interviews I've done with kids have often been boring because they have nothing to talk about and can't be drawn out."

A word of caution

Only one employer thought that there might be negative aspects arising from placements. She advised caution in assessing whether a work experience scheme was beneficial or not, because it depended very much on the kinds of activities pupils did and how they were treated.

"A bad work experience programme where they're left completely alone or are molly-coddled doesn't teach them anything. They get a completely wrong idea of work. So it has to be a good work experience programme where it's treated as though it's work and they're proper recruits."

Pupils' experience on placement

We were interested in knowing what types of activities pupils were given and whether they were treated in a similar way to full−time trainees. Employers were also asked about the kind of training and supervision that they had been able to provide and about any information they had given the students on recruitment, necessary qualifications and interviews. Finally, we asked whether any of the placements had led in the past to offers of employment.

Placement activities

In the vast majority of cases, pupils were given the same kinds of tasks as a trainee would be, although it was often necessary to tailor activities to allow for the limited length of the placements, the confidentiality of material pupils might come across, and restrictions imposed by youngsters not being allowed to use certain equipment (for instance, cash registers or heavy duty floor polishers).

Placements were all said to be practically based (ie the pupils 'doing' rather than simply observing) and employers tried to ensure that the youngsters were given a broad range of activities.

"We try to give them a range of activities . . . we don't want to use them just as messengers. We want to give them a chance to work: to see how to work in an office

9

and to see what people actually do once they've passed the stage of being a junior."

Only two organisations admittedly treated pupils differently from new recruits: one was a primary school and the other a construction firm. In the primary school it was left to each teacher to decide how best to use the youngsters in the classroom. Usually activities involved working with reading groups, helping in the painting corner or playing games with the young children. In the construction firm pupils were assigned to different tasks depending on their abilities and interests. This organisation put a lot of effort into constructing a realistic project for youngsters to work on.

> "I always try to have some sort of point to the week, so they have a goal, so there's an element of training, of putting that training into use and then achieving a result. I try to look at the child and say 'What would be right for that person?' and I try to make it open ended so that the pace isn't forced . . . and they have a chance to achieve something at the end of it."

This firm had strong feelings about how the work experience scheme should be tackled and the types of activities pupils should be given.

> "I gather in some places the pupils are just given sweeping up or making tea. They don't get that here. We want them to get work experience. They're here to learn what business is about and to have their eyes opened to work."

Training and supervision

In most cases there was little formal training as such. Instead, pupils were given a short talk on that particular organisation and then were trained on-the-job by actually 'doing'. They tended to be allocated to a supervisor or more experienced worker whom they worked alongside.

> "It seemed a wee bit pointless to try and spend the whole week training them. We wanted them to get a chance to do something. The job wasn't that difficult in real terms . . . it's just really getting to know what they have to do and then doing it. So they're really just working alongside someone else being shown what to do and being left to get on with it."

One firm tried to arrange advance interviews for all the pupils who were to go there on placement. This provided the youngsters with the opportunity to look round and to ask any questions before they started their week's work. It also gave the firm the chance to see what the pupils were like.

> "I am able to tell them how to come dressed to work, what type of shoes to wear for the sales floor. If there was someone who I wasn't happy about . . . I'd contact the school and say 'Look, I'm not happy, I don't agree with so-and-so and I'd rather she didn't come in' . . . [in my previous store] we really sort of vetted them and it saved any problems when they did actually came along to us."

A second employer, the construction firm mentioned earlier, not only tried to incorporate an element of training into the placement but also interviewed their pupils at the end of the week.

> ". . . we pretended they were being interviewed for the job they had been doing all week and asked questions on it . . . Afterwards we gave them a verbal and written report on how they had done at the interview."

A few of the firms gave a brief induction training which covered the basics of the job and, in a limited number of organisations, health and safety.

> "We start off by not only giving them a job description of what they're going to have to do but also a safety booklet about keeping safe on the site. They're told not to do anything silly and our people are told not to push them."

At one organisation offering clerical placements, they tended to take the opportunity of any quiet times to explain the operation of modern office equipment (like word processors).

In all of the firms the pupils, although not always under close supervision, were never left completely on their own and there was always someone available to help the pupils if they had any difficulties.

> "We do as much supervising as we can. We hope, though, that they'll use their initiative and if they're stuck they'll ask. We'll then give as much help as we can."

Recruitment advice and jobs

In twelve of the organisations pupils were given no formal

information about job applications because it was assumed that the school would provide such advice. However, a number said that they would do this if asked to by the school. It was also suggested that the staff with whom the pupils worked on the placements may have given them such advice or would have answered any questions youngsters asked.

"That [information] would only be given to them if they showed an interest and said they'd like to be a checkout operator or something. Then the Section Head or Manager would approach us for the best way to go about this. We'd usually advise them to apply for YTS."

"Not officially, but the staff usually take them in hand and advise them."

It was suggested to the pupils by two of the firms that they should obtain application forms nearer the time they were to leave school. A third firm had given similar advice and had also indicated that part-time out-of-school-hours work might be available. Recruitment information from one of the local authority institutions had been in terms of pointing out to the pupils that district council policy was to recruit through the YTS.

A veterinary surgeon made a point of telling pupils of the problems connected with getting a job in a veterinary practice but suggested that if they were really interested they should write individual letters to all vets in the city.

One organisation, the construction firm mentioned earlier, said they gave quite systematic information about recruitment.

"We give them information on CITB apprenticeships. Also the boys who are more academic can talk to our Company Secretary about how to become a CA. We can arrange for any of the pupils to talk to people working in the appropriate section and can also make contacts for them outside."

Several of the employers had given students general informal advice on the skills and prerequisites necessary for undertaking either that particular type of work or on getting a job in general.

"We try to tell them about presenting themselves properly — not to have your hands in your pockets, to be clean and tidy and smart. These types of things that are the best way of selling yourself."

"They didn't seem to realise the importance of correct typing in an office. They saw it as an exercise, like they'd do at school, where someone points out your mistakes and it's okay. I tried to explain that if you're sending out a letter to someone it's got to look good and be tidy and correct."

It was also pointed out to the youngsters that the skills and experience they had gained on placements and the insights made would be equally relevant to other organisations.

Two of the interviewees expressed doubts about the wisdom of raising the issue of recruitment and qualifications with the students because it might suggest that jobs were readily available when in fact this was far from the case.

Although the purpose of the work experience programme is not to find permanent employment for the pupils, we nevertheless wondered whether, in the past, any of the pupils had been offered a post as a result of placements. Four of the employers had, in the past, offered full-time places to the work experience pupils from the school. (One of the offers had not been taken up because the youngster concerned was too young to leave school until the winter term of S5. Negotiations were still taking place to try to ensure that he did not lose the opportunity). Eight pupils were taken on under the Youth Training Scheme by the other three organisations and one of these was later taken on as an apprentice.

A number of employers expressed regret that appropriate vacancies had not arisen.

"This is a small office and we don't have a junior. The work experience scheme has made us start talking about seeing what's involved in taking on a YTS person. But we have a stable secretarial staff and in [an office of this type] you don't always know what the future workload will be and whether there will be enough work for another person."

The value of work experience for pupils: employers' views

Clearly there would be no point in organising work experience for young people unless it was of value to them. We will consider later what the pupils themselves saw as valuable but what was the view of the employers?

An insight into a particular trade

First, giving pupils an insight into a particular occupation could reinforce a young person's career choice or, alternatively and equally valuable, it could show them that they were not suited to the particular type of work.

"They do appreciate the reasons they're being sent out —
to give them a basic idea of what it's like to work in a
shop. Some have said 'I don't really know if I want to
work in a shop, but I have the opportunity to come here
and see what it's like'. And talking to them on their last
day they either said 'Yes, great, I enjoyed it and I now
know you have to do this and I didn't know there was so
much involved in dealing with customers.' And others
maybe are a wee bit disappointed with what they've seen
and they realise that they don't have the patience to deal
with customers and to do that type of job."

The realities of the workplace

Almost equally as important as gaining more knowledge about a
particular job was, in the employers' eyes, learning about the
realities of a workplace in general and the discipline involved in
work.

"It lets them see what work is like. They are subject to
the same rules as everyone else and it's explained what's
expected of them and the pressures there are at work.
The reasons for the rules are also explained: that your
actions can affect other people . . . They have to learn to
see the effects on other people; for instance, that leaving
your post can hold up other peoples' production and can
affect their bonuses. They have to learn they're working
as a team."

"Instead of blinkers about industry, you're giving them
binoculars — you give the kids an insight into what
happens in the workplace."

Pupils were able to see that the age hierarchy that operated at
school (with older people having more responsibility and power)
was not necessarily the norm at work. In shops, in particular,
there were often young supervisors who were in charge of older
sales assistants.

A few of the employers expressed fears that because their
particular organisations were rather atypical (for instance, very
informal, or a co-operative), pupils might assume that all
workplaces were similar. These interviewees made a point of
telling pupils that other firms operated on a different basis and
that behaviour acceptable in their own business might not be
acceptable in others.

Pupils' self development

In addition to gaining an insight into work practices, there were also seen to be benefits in terms of self-development. The youngsters were being put in situations where they were working with adults who treated them as fellow employees. They were able to see themselves, therefore, in a more adult light and to gain a sense of responsibility.

"... I think for the first time they're being treated as adults. I think just going into a work environment and doing something with someone who is working there all the time is what they enjoy most."

"[Working in a primary school] they're grown up as far as the wee ones are concerned and it's quite good for their confidence if they can see themselves in this more adult role."

The sheer mechanics of getting to the workplace and having to talk to and get on with strangers was seen as a method of broadening the pupils' outlook and providing them with the opportunity to gain confidence.

"The pupils gain confidence. Having to find the place, having to come in the door and knowing what to say at the reception desk can all be daunting. Having done that they've achieved something and it also teaches them how to do it in future."

"They meet working people; they meet folk of different types and creeds — people they wouldn't meet at school. It all helps to broaden their outlook."

"The two [pupils] we had were quite quiet chaps and here they saw the usual Glaswegian habit of 'slagging off'. It helps them realise that it's not all heads down and that there is banter. Towards the end of the week they were coming out of themselves a lot. Dealing with the public is a good thing too — initially, everyone is frightened about it. The pupils learned to be more at ease with the public."

An aid to getting a job

Only two of the interviewees mentioned that the work experience placements might serve in some way as an aid to getting a job. Having had experience of working in a shop, for example, might make that pupil preferable in an employer's eyes to someone without experience. The week's placements would also provide the pupils with something to use on their curriculum vitae and could act as a important discussion point at an interview.

Employers' impressions of the pupils

Pupils differ in ability, manner and the degree of commitment that they show and these qualities may affect the way that employers view work experience programmes and the schools involved. A firm's inclination to take part in future schemes may be influenced both by bad experiences with youngsters and, alternatively, by good pupil attitudes. We, therefore, asked interviewees about their general impressions of the pupils, about any problems they had encountered and whether anything had particularly impressed them about the youngsters.

General impressions

None of the employers' general impressions of the pupils were negative, and ten expressed strong positive reactions. These included statements such as "The kids were great", "very good", "they got on very well" and "they were very interested". A further five described pupils as "working well", "good", "fine" or "nice". Several of the interviewees said that, although there had been differences between the pupils in terms of confidence and initiative, they had been "pleasantly surprised" at the pupils' willingness to learn, their behaviour, their appearance and their time keeping.

> "I think they've done very well. I've had no problems. They could be cheeky to me if they wanted because its no skin off their nose . . . I've been quite surprised really because I thought I'd have a wee bit of bother with it — maybe a couple not doing what they're told. But there's been none of that."

Interestingly, a few of the employers wondered whether, since they had experienced no problems with the youngsters, the school had handpicked those pupils who were better behaved. This, in fact, was not the case and only eight youngsters from the whole year group were not or would not have been allowed to go out on placement because of behavioural problems. As Ms B, the teacher who organised places, put it "on the question were only the 'good pupils' allowed out . . . we don't have 86 guaranteed super-reliable, mature, polite pupils!"

Only three of the interviewees were more reserved in their opinion of the students. They described them as "average", "okay" or "our reports on them are not unfavourable but not glowing either."

Problems encountered

There had been no problems at all with the pupils in fourteen of the eighteen workplaces, and a further three employers said that there had not been any major problems.

A number of the interviewees pointed out that there had to be an element of trust with the youngsters and that this trust had not been abused.

"We've an open surgery and have a cash box lying about but we've never had any problems."

Even pupils whom the school had been uncertain about had proved satisfactory.

"I know one girl who came down. [The school] was a bit concerned about her because she was very shy and her reading wasn't very good. But she was actually a very nice girl and she came out of her shell. We were really very pleased with her at the end of the day."

The inappropriateness of manner of some of the boys when dealing with customers caused minor problems, as did the two pupils who left before the end of the week.

"We had one boy last week who didn't come back on the Thursday and Friday. He was very quiet. We couldn't get much communication out of him. [His work mates] were exhausted after the first day trying to stimulate some kind of conversation from him."

"The only thing that bothers me is the ones who don't last — I'm wondering what I did wrong and am feeling sorry that I didn't get through. But it's work experience for me too, learning that you've got to be there listening and letting them know you'll be there listening."

The one employer who had experienced a major problem (in the past) with a pupil from the school said that he had had to send a boy back to school because he simply was not interested.

"The laddie obviously showed enthusiasm for a job in the retail trade before he came down but all of a sudden when he came down and saw that he had to dirty his hands, he started getting a bit stroppy, saying 'I'm no' doing that, I'm no' getting paid' .....So I just sent him back."

This interviewee, however, realised that it had been an isolated incident and, because his other placements had worked out well, had not been deterred from taking part in future programmes.

One staff manager had encountered a case of stealing by a work experience pupil from *another* school. She said that the incident had changed the store manager's attitude to taking part in such schemes and that it "took several months to persuade him to try again and that the incident had been a one-off situation." In addition, she now tells pupils:

> ". . . what gross misconduct is and what will happen. It's stressed that should they be tempted to take something, we'll just follow the procedure [of prosecuting] . . . I put across very strongly what would happen and how it'd affect them and their future."

Another staff manager had experienced problems with four pupils from another school-based project who had gone there on placements the week after the pupils from the case-study school. These pupils had caused such difficulties with other staff (because of bad language, laziness, poor customer relations and religious bigotry) that they had been asked to leave after only four days of their three week placements. Although that store was still willing to accept pupils for placements, it was decided that all students to be sent through that particular scheme would be interviewed first and would be rejected if the personnel officer had any doubts about them.

Favourable impressions

When asked if anything had particularly impressed them about the pupils, five replied that nothing had. On the other hand, six of the employers made mention of a pupil who had shown special promise in their line of work.

> "There was one boy this week who I reckon would be a natural as a bricklayer. His brick wall was spot on. He'd done it with a level and that showed he was keen. Another boy last year could work on anything you gave him."

Willingness, enthusiasm, initiative and the ability to get on with other staff and the public were qualities which attracted favourable comment from employers.

> "I was really impressed that they were interested and the interest was there right from the beginning . . . They did show a lot of enthusiasm . . . At the end of the day I'll spend as much time as I can with someone like that."

> "She was very good and settled in very quickly. She did things on her own initiative, like looking after clients. She would go to the customer and talk and communicate easily. She was very, very good."

"They were quite confident, but quietly so. They were enthusiastic and were taking in what was being said. They weren't just here for a skive from school. They did want to get involved — which is better for the trainer. The supervisors thoroughly enjoyed the time with them and felt they got through to them."

Evidence of the pupils' enthusiasm was given by two of the employers. In one workplace (a charity), the pupil who was with them offered to come back in to work voluntarily if they were ever busy. And in a second, a pupil asked after her first week if she could continue to work for a second week — the school October holiday week.

Employers were particularly impressed when pupils showed initiative by asking questions about what they were doing or by asking for work to do rather than waiting for it to be given to them.

"[He] was a fireball — desperate to do something. He'd ask 'Did I do it right?' or 'What do I do next?' It was quite gratifying that you have some youngsters who're interested in employment."

"They both showed a bit of initiative and would ask if there was anything they could do rather than sitting doing nothing. They tried to be useful. I thought this was good because at that age they're very shy and don't ask."

Initiative can be shown in a number of ways as the following employer pointed out:

"At the end of the week, not only did the pupils do their [work] but they also realised what kind of people we were — they bought us sticky buns for afternoon tea . . . I wrote in my report of them: 'They were a very effervescent group. The trio bought us sticky buns for tea break . . . showing not only initiative but keen observation of our weaknesses' . . . We were all moved by that. It proved we'd got it to work."

Employers' views of the scheme itself

We were interested in finding out how satisfied employers were with the scheme in terms of, firstly, the role of the school, and secondly the length of placements. We also wondered whether interviewees felt that any changes should be made to the scheme.

The role of the school

The success of a work experience programme depends not only

on the pupils and the employers but also on the schools. Schools have the key tasks of preparing the youngsters for their week's experience and for maintaining contact with and giving support to the work providers. If these are not carried out successfully the other groups can become disillusioned and the experience prove unprofitable. With this in mind, we asked the interviewees their opinions about the way in which the pupils had been prepared and about the support available to the firm from the school.

Pupil preparation

The majority of interviewees said that, although they had little idea about what kind of preparation had gone on in the school before the pupils went out on work experience, they felt that there had been some and that it had been adequate since they had encountered few problems.

"I think because we haven't had any problems, it's been okay. [The pupils] have not come looking for more than they got."

Mention was also made of the fact that pupils had arrived dressed in suitable clothing, had the appropriate equipment and knew about arrangements for lunch and the hours to be worked. This was cited as evidence of preparation on the part of the school.

"The school issues them with safety boots and overalls so they come ready equipped. So they must have given them some sort of insight in health and safety."

One participant was particularly impressed with the preparation that pupils had received.

"The school obviously put a lot of work and thought into this because the kids were well prepared and could find their way on buses . . . quite clearly the parents must be backing it well too or otherwise the kids wouldn't come so well turned out and organised with things like sandwiches."

Some of the employers were impressed that a teacher had contacted them before the pupils were sent out in order to find out what was expected of placement students.

A number commented sympathetically on the difficulties involved for schools in preparing pupils for specific work placements.

"Unless their teachers have worked in a hairdresser they

can't really prepare them. And anyway standards probably vary between hairdressers."

"I think the school's hands are tied as to what they can do to prepare them for work experience. After all, they'd be preparing them for a period of preparation for work. I think they're going the right way about it in that they're giving them the opportunity of work experience."

A few interviewees, however, thought that there were areas in which preparation could be improved. One office manager believed that schools should ensure that pupils who were undertaking clerical placements were able to type and should have experience of modern office equipment. It was also felt that students should be made to understand the importance of following instructions.

"They should have been prepared for the discipline and effort required. Discipline has to be highlighted because youngsters [in general] take it very badly that they have to do what the supervisors say."

(However, the project organisers see teaching youngsters about the discipline of work as difficult if it is not undertaken within a relevant context. Thus work experience itself is viewed as an important means by which the requirements of the work situation are learned by the students.)

Finally, one employer thought that the schools really did not know what they were preparing pupils for. He thought that it would be worthwhile for teachers to approach different employers to see what they are looking for in youngsters and then to use that information as the basis for student preparation.

School support of employers

All of the employers were satisfied with the support given to them by the school. They liked the fact that the schools gave them advance warning of when pupils were coming out on placements and that a teacher either visited the students during their week's work experience or phoned to see how they were getting on. It was felt that there was little more that the teachers could do and that if the schools did intervene more it would detract from the independence of the pupils.

"The teacher does come in and have a look from time to time to make sure that no one's being abused or it's not slave labour. I don't think the school can do much more quite frankly. I think the kids are trying to find their own way in the world and this is phase one of being pushed out the nest and having to find your own way."

Most of the interviewees had not come across any problems and so had not needed additional support. However, they were impressed with the liaison teacher, Ms B, and felt confident that should any problems arise she would provide all the help necessary.

"She [Ms B] has been very good. She's been first rate. The school seems to appreciate what we're doing. I imagine they'd be very supportive if needed."

The employers also felt that the use of assessment forms which they completed for each pupil meant that the school would get a clear picture of what was happening during placements and, similarly, the reports written by pupils gave the firm an idea of the students' views.

Only two criticisms were made about the role of the school. The first concerned a plea for employers to be given more information about what it was hoped that pupils would gain from work experience and about where placements fitted into the rest of the curriculum. This information should include the activities the school would like the students to do and the type of expectations the school had about what the pupils would learn. One staff manager said that she would like to know what the end product of the whole module was and what type of follow-up there was at school.

"It hasn't really been fully explained to us what its aims are. What happens when they get back to school? Is our report filed away or do they go over it with the pupils?"

The second criticism or suggestion (which is clearly in conflict with one of the points made above) related to the need for more visits by the teacher to pupils out on work experience.

"I'd really like to see them visit the children more. They do try to make an effort to visit every child but it's very difficult to do this . . . It's helpful for us and I think it's important we have a good relationship with the schools and the school sees what goes on. And it's good for the teacher to get the chance to go out into industry to see what's happening — something they might not normally get to do."

The length of placements

Although the work experience placements tended to last for one week, other schemes, such as Project Trident, believe that a block period of three weeks is the minimum needed for:

> . . . a young person of this age to settle into a strange environment, make proper working relationships with fellow workers and supervisors, learn to do a worthwhile job adequately, accept the routines and disciplines of the workplace, and enjoy a full sense of achievement, in being a productive and responsible member of a working group. (Kerry, 1983)

We wondered, therefore, what the employers' views were on the adequacy of the time pupils spent on placements.

Seven of the interviewees felt that a week was sufficient because it allowed pupils to gain basic skills and to learn about work practices without becoming bored. It was also felt by the employers that:

> "[The pupils] can't afford to loose much more time from school — they need the things they're learning at school. And from the employer's point of view a week is as much time as they can give voluntarily. To ask them to give up more than that is too much."

A further two interviewees thought that although a week was adequate, it could easily be extended to a fortnight; and a third felt that although a week was as much as an employer could give, from the pupils' point of view it was not sufficient.

Eight of the work providers stated that a week was not long enough: five thought the scheme should be extended to a fortnight (although one said that the extra week should not be compulsory because some pupils may have found during their first week that they did not like the work); two suggested a two to four week period and one advocated a three to four week block.

A longer timespan was seen as necessary because it was felt that just as pupils were beginning to settle in and gain confidence their placements ended. An extension would allow a slower pace and mean that students were able to gain a wider understanding of work practices and to learn to use their initiative.

> "It takes two weeks to show them the full routine so a week's not long enough for them to get really involved and to learn it."

> "When we did work experience in the store I worked in previously, we did start off with one week and I felt we were trying to cram in an awful lot in that week. The girls weren't having as great an understanding of what we

were asking them to do as they would if they were there longer. We found a two week period was better for the trainee and the supervisor."

It was also felt that often a week was not long enough for firms to assess pupils properly.

"It's not particularly easy to assess someone in one week. You've got to think of the settling-in period when maybe they are not performing as well as they could had they been with us for longer."

Changes to the work experience scheme

When specifically asked whether they would like to see any changes made to the work experience scheme, ten of the employers said that they would. Eight of their suggestions for change were concerned with extending the length of time that pupils were out on placement. As mentioned above, about half of the interviewees thought that the programme should last between two weeks to a month, rather than for one week only.

Only two suggestions were not concerned with the length of placements. One (already discussed) related to the need for inculcating a sense of the discipline of work in pupils before they were sent out. The other expressed concern that the school should ensure that students were really interested in that type of work before giving them placements in a particular organisation.

"It amazed me that someone coming to an office couldn't type. I wondered if there should have been more communication to see if she really wanted to be in an office and if so, why she couldn't type."

During the course of the interviews, three employers suggested that the scheme would prove more valuable to pupils if they had a number of placements in different organisations. These placements could either be concerned with the same type of work (for instance, placements in a number of different stores) or each one with completely different aspects of work (eg one week in a shop, another in a factory, a third in the building trade). This variety of experience would introduce pupils to the different work practices present in different firms and help to prevent students assuming that what happened in one placement was common to all organisations involved in the same type of work. However, as we shall see later, the school's ability to do this is severely limited by timetabling constraints.

3

PUPILS' VIEWS OF WORK EXPERIENCE

Work experience is generally thought to be a 'good thing'. It is seen as aiding pupils' transition from school to adult life by giving them a taste of the world of relationships and work outside school. But what do pupils feel about it and what are the effects of work experience?

Although we had intended to tap the pupils' experience in a number of ways (detailed in Appendix III), analysis of the data derived through these other methods showed that they lacked the richness and detail of information obtained during the interviews. This section is therefore based largely on interviews with 18 of the students.

Pupils' perceptions of, and reactions to, work experience are presented in two parts. The first focusses on the pupils' views (expressed during the interviews) on aspects of work experience. The second part provides a short summary of the non-interview data on the pupils' views of the usefulness and effects of work experience.

Pupils were asked for their views on: the school's organisation of the scheme; the placements; reasons for participation in the scheme (for both the employers and the students themselves); their experiences of work experience; what they had learned from placements; their other experiences of work; and their future career intentions.

School organisation of work experience

Choice and allocation of placements

Before placements were allocated, pupils were given a form describing the types available. It asked them to rank their first three choices and to tick any others which they would be willing to consider. Youngsters who were within twelve months of the minimum school leaving age could select placements from employer *or* community based workplaces. Younger pupils, who were not eligible to leave school until the end of the winter term in their fifth year, were not legally allowed to go out on work experience and so were given a choice of community placements instead.

Ten of the students interviewed were allocated to the placements of their first choice, five to their second choice and three to their third. Only two students made complaints about the range of options that had been available to them. One of these was an older pupil who did not get her first choice of placement and would have preferred to work with children; and the second was a younger pupil who had wanted to go out on a hairdressing placement.

School's preparation of pupils

Work experience is one part of a larger 'introduction to work' programme whose main component is the 'Work Course'. The course, consisting of work-related modules, lasts for 10 weeks and, because of timetabling problems, involves only a third of the fourth year at one time. The first group begins the course in August, the second in November and the last in February. The course should complement work experience and should provide both preparation and follow-up for the placements, but because of the timing this has not been the case for many of the pupils.

The initial preparation for work experience had taken place in the summer term of third year when, as the teacher in charge (Ms B) explained:

> "All the pupils . . . were asked to fill in a questionnaire stating (a) 2 jobs they would like to get; (b) 2 kinds of work experience they would like to go on. (The latter question was in case the answer to the first was the Navy and the Oil Rigs, and its purpose was made clear on the form.) The results of the questionnaire were the basis on which I tried to get appropriate placements set up."

In S4, the Work Course, for the reasons outlined above, was not available to the majority of the pupils before they went out on placement. Instead, most students had only two preparatory meetings. The first was concerned with explaining what work experience was, when it would be and that the purpose was not to find permanent jobs for the pupils. This discussion also covered appropriate behaviour — honesty and politeness, time-keeping, being friendly, and that workmates liked to be asked questions. The option forms, which were to be shown to parents, were given out and the teacher went through them, explaining what the different placements were. Finally, pupils were given information about how to fill in a curriculum vitae for the work experience employers. The purpose of the second meeting was to go over the placements allocated, to whom to report, information about travel refunds etc. It was essentially 'mechanical preparation' although the teacher tried to include some information about what youngsters could gain from work experience, what it was like and the things to think about. In addition to this preparation, however, certain pupils whose behaviour Guidance teachers or Ms B were dubious about were all interviewed separately and at some length by Ms B.

> "The substance of the interview was that their behaviour was not always good but we wanted to give them a chance *but* they must behave well etc. and I asked them to guarantee to me (just verbally) that they would." (Ms B)

Ms B realised that such preparation was not ideal and would have preferred, had time been available, to have taken pupils in smaller groups and given more information about the intentions of work experience rather than just the practical arrangements. She is considering, for future years, trying to see pupils in their last term of third year to talk about work in general and work experience in particular.

The timing of the Work Course also created major problems in terms of arranging follow-up discussions to build on and consolidate the work experiences. Most of the follow-up work was intended to be done during the Work Course but, again because of the timetabling problems, there was sometimes a lack of synchronisation between the course and the placements. This meant that a third of S4 received a good preparation from the course before they went on placement but had no follow-up from it. The second group of S4 received no preparation from the course but had a fairly immediate follow-up. For the final group the course was not available until 2-2½ months after their placements and was, as a consequence, very belated.

However, all of the pupils did receive some immediate follow-up: Ms B saw each pupil individually after the week's placement so that she could go over the reports employers had written about them although this was only a very brief discussion. She also spent one period with the 'O' Grade English pupils after their work experience. This was mainly used for writing their reports for the employers. The non-certificate English pupils did this with their English teacher.

The lack of articulation between the Work Course and the placements is, in our view, the main deficiency in the school's work experience programme. However, Ms B is well aware of the problems that this has created and is trying to arrange that, in subsequent years, the Work Course consists of one double period throughout the whole session, providing time for both more detailed preparation and more immediate follow-up.

Given the lack of detailed preparation, it is surprising that the vast majority of pupils (15) did not feel that their preparation for work experience had been inadequate and in fact, two made the point that:

"It was work experience so we should find out for ourselves."

Of the other three students, two felt that although the preparation had been "okay", they should have been told about exactly where the workplace was and more about the conditions of work (eg "that it was a typing pool rather than a little office".) The third felt that the information that they had been given was not detailed enough and that they should have known more about what to expect and what they would be doing on placements.

Length and timing of placements

As seen earlier, employers were almost equally divided in their opinions as to the best length of work experience. The pupils also held differing views on the ideal length but were less equally divided. Some of the school organisers of the scheme had predicted that pupils would want longer placements but, in fact, only seven of the 18 students held this view. The other eleven felt that a week had been "just right". Some of this latter group were worried about school work missed during placement. One pupil summed up the dilemma:

"It would have been better if it [work experience] had been longer but if it was two weeks that would be too long because we'd be missing too much [school] work."

All of those who thought that a week was too short, felt that two weeks would have been better. They believed that a fortnight would have given them more experience and it would have solved the problem of them just beginning to know their "way around" when they had to leave.

Some pupils also felt that the timing of placements — just a few weeks before the 'Prelims' for the certificate examinations — had created difficulties. They suggested that placements should be arranged during January instead. However the organiser, Ms B, illustrated the amount of thought that had been given to the timing and the pros and cons associated with different periods throughout the academic year:

"a. A great number of our pupils leave at the end of May of their fourth year. Therefore to use June of S4 as many schools do would mean that many were never offered work experience . . . [so] it had to be located somewhere in S4.

b. Staff would understandably not like pupils going out in small groups throughout the year. To send them all out at one time was much less disruptive to their school work.

c. January or February . . . shops and hotels told us not to use these months because they were too quiet and also shops used them for stock-taking . . . construction firms also warned us off this period because of cold weather problems. Staff have opposed it because January-March work after the Prelims is seen as a very important time. March unacceptable because too near 'O' Grades.

d. This left the first term of S4. It could not happen as soon as school started because there had to be time for contact with the pupils . . . and then to send the information, CVs etc. on to employers. The last week of September and first of October were thought of but were only 4-day weeks because of the Friday/Monday September holiday. Therefore the two weeks chosen were the earliest I could manage. All pupils had returned, in fact, five full weeks before the Prelims started.

e. It was decided to offer the younger group work experience at the same time as the older group as community-based experience was thought to be valid. Those who are to leave in December of S5 will be offered the opportunity to go out on employer-based work experience in the October of that year. Some will miss out then because of Highers commitments and I hope to run a small scheme for them in the June following their Highers."

Changes to the work experience scheme

Ten of the pupils suggested changes that could be made to the scheme. Four repeated that it should be extended to two weeks and two others were concerned that some of the youngsters out on work experience had not worked the full working day.

"Everyone should work the normal work hours — not 9-4 because that's just the normal school hours. And although it is a different atmosphere it's not the same as working the proper work hours."

The other suggestions for change were really complaints from the pupils. One student thought that they should have been paid, another felt that she should have been allowed to wear trousers to work and a third, younger, pupil was annoyed that she had to take a community rather than work placement. The final complaint was from a boy who had been bored by the frequent periods of inactivity. He said that the school should have ensured that there was plenty to do on placements.

The placements

From the pupil's point of view, the value and enjoyment of work experience depends to a large extent on the type of activities given to do, the help available and relationships with other staff. We, therefore, asked questions about all these matters and also included one concerned with the advice employers had given about aspects of getting a job.

Placement activities, supervision and advice

The majority of pupils felt (as had the employers) that they were given the same kinds of tasks as other workers, and all said that they were participating in rather than simply observing work activities. However, five of the youngsters believed that their work was different from that done by the other staff. One of these said that the work was broadly similar except when there was not much to do.

> "The supervisor said we could try this paper out. So we'd to sit and type it in our own time. It was the exam paper that you had to pass to get a job there."

Of the other four who said that their work was different, three confirmed what their employers had said: two, in a construction firm, were given a project to do; and one (placed in a primary school) was helping the teacher. The other pupil, who was working in a supermarket, complained that, although she had been able to work for a day and a half in the delicatessen, the rest of her time was spent collecting trolleys from areas of the store. She felt that such a task provided her with no useful experience and had also isolated her from the other staff.

All of the pupils were shown by a member of staff what to do and there was always someone available if they ran into difficulties.

Fifteen of those interviewed had received no advice about job interviews or about how to obtain work in that or similar workplaces. None of the pupils mentioned the informal advice on appearance, manner etc that the employers said they had given (see page 12). It is possible that the way in which we put this question to students made them assume that we were referring to formal advice. Alternatively it is possible that such advice (because of its informal nature) was not really internalised by the youngsters. In addition, the systematic information about

30

recruitment that one firm said that it gave was not mentioned by the two pupils interviewed who had had placements there.

The three pupils who mentioned that they had received some information on 'getting a job' said that:

> "They said if we worked well and Saturday jobs came up they would let us know."

> "She said if I liked that type of work the only thing to do was to apply for the YTS first."

> "He did say if we were going for a job we should tell them about our work experience."

Other staff

Seventeen of the youngsters said that they had got on either very well or quite well with the other staff; the odd pupil out said that since she was working in a school she only really met the one person she was working with (whom she thought was "okay"). The pupils found the other staff helpful and several felt that they had been treated like a normal worker.

> "They were very nice and very helpful and didn't make me feel out of place . . . when we went up to the canteen they introduced you to everyone and didn't make you feel left out."

> "They treated us the same as everyone else. Some didn't even know — they thought I was working there."

> "It was a good chance to mingle with professional people, who, unlike at school, treat you like an adult."

Reasons for participation in work experience

We asked pupils about two different aspects of reasons for participation. Firstly, their views on why they thought employers had taken part in the scheme, and, secondly, what the pupils thought they themselves would gain from the experience.

Employer participation

The reasons given by pupils for employer participation fell into three main categories: explicitly altruistic reasons; tangible benefits for the firm; and reasons which fell in between.

A third of the pupils made mention of altruistic motives: employers just felt like helping youngsters to find out about work.

> "I don't think there really is any benefit — maybe they just wanted to help out."

31

"To help pupils find out what it's like to work in a big store like that . . . They get pleasure out of it by helping young people like us — they're getting that."

Tangible benefits for the particular firm were mentioned by just over a third. Three said that it was a method of finding new employees; two stated that they were working on a project which the company wanted to test the feasibility of ; one believed that work experience was a way of getting extra work done; and the last, who was placed in a library, felt that it was a method of getting youngsters interested in the library.

Interestingly, many (but not all) of the pupils who saw tangible gains for firms were echoing the views expressed by their particular employers (see page 6).

The remaining motives assigned to employers participation were concerned with letting pupils see what a particular type of work was like, giving them an opportunity to work with adults, and helping students to prepare themselves for their working lives. In contrast to the employers' views, pupils were much more likely to place emphasis on the purpose of a company's participation being to give students an insight into a *particular* job rather than into work practices in *general*. However, overall, pupils seemed to have fairly accurate perceptions of employers' motives.

Pupil participation

When asked about the purpose of work experience, pupils once again showed themselves to be very perceptive. None of those interviewed thought that it would lead directly to a job. Most of the youngsters saw the value of the scheme in very similar terms to those expressed by the employers: to give an idea of what a particular job or trade was like and to learn about the realities of what was involved in working life.

Work experience was seen as helping pupils learn about specific jobs by giving them the chance to get an idea of what that particular job involved and whether they were able to cope with that kind of work. It was also seen as giving them more information on which to decide their futures.

"You can find out if you like that kind of work and if you want to do it when you leave school."

"In future I want to work in an office and on work experience I learned some important things about office equipment. Also I was told when you start as an office junior you would be expected to make the tea and other odd jobs. So if I get an office job I won't be too disappointed if I have to do these things because I have already been warned about them."

Other pupils learned the equally valuable lesson that they did not like that particular type of work.

"I didn't like [. . .]. I wouldn't like to work there."

Work experience was also frequently seen as a means of preparing pupils for work in general by giving them an idea of what it would be like.

"Even if the place didn't appeal to the pupil at least it gave them some idea of what work was like."

Two of the pupils felt that they were now better prepared to deal with "first day nerves".

Many of the pupils talked about more specific aspects of preparation for work. A large number mentioned having experience of working with adults.

"You find out what it is like working with adults or people just a little older than you."

Getting used to the working day, travelling, learning to get up early and finding out about the need for time keeping were also seen as important.

"It gets you used to getting up early for work and the work hours and getting you used to working with a group of people."

A fair number of pupils mentioned that the experience could be used when applying for future jobs.

"If you get a good reference and you're going for an interview that would be an advantage because they'll know you've done work experience and were good at it and might not ask you so much."

A few pupils, although stating that the purpose of work experience was to help them to learn about daily working life, felt that because they had not learned any new skills they had not benefited from their placements.

"I learned nothing at [. . .] because I knew how to make beds and clean the rooms."

"I don't think it would help me at all because anybody can price goods and put them on shelves."

It could be that, although it was pointed out in school that the main purpose of work experience was not to learn a lot of *specific* skills but rather to learn about working life in general, these pupils saw the putting into practice of specific skills as being the chief indicator of having achieved and learned something.

Pupils' experiences of work experience

This section is concerned with the pupils' subjective experiences of work experience — whether they enjoyed their work, what they had been worried about beforehand and whether they had had any problems.

Enjoyment

Fifteen of the youngsters expressed no reservations about having enjoyed their work experience. The most common reason given was having enjoyed working with the other staff.

> "It's better than in school. In school you're treated much younger because you're the pupil, but there you're treated the same as the rest."

> "I enjoyed being at work because it made me feel very grown up. I felt like I was one of the staff which had worked there for years, it felt like home." (Taken from a pupil's log book).

Other reasons for having enjoyed the experience were that the work itself was interesting, that there was always something to do and that time was spent outside the classroom doing "real work". It also provided the youngsters with the opportunity to consolidate what they already knew and to organise their knowledge in a more structured manner.

> "I've always enjoyed working on my bike and helping my uncle on his motor. Working there, I learned what the things were called that I was doing — before I was just doing them at random."

The three pupils who were less enthusiastic about their experience had enjoyed some parts but had been bored when there had been nothing to do.

> "Sometimes it was boring because you ran out of things to do . . . You're told to clean out the storeroom and you take your time because you know there'll be nothing to do afterwards. And sometimes it really drags because you're doing nothing."

A few other minor difficulties emerged from the questionnaire responses. Not knowing anyone in the workplace and not seeing friends bothered two pupils and a third, who was placed in a primary school, felt ill at ease with the teachers.

> "I was very tierd [sic] at the end of each day. I also felt very inferieor [sic] to the teachers."

Surprisingly, only three pupils complained about not being paid.

> "We should have been doing a *real* job and getting paid for it instead of doing our own little project."

Other students talked about specific negative aspects of the job they had been doing. One pupil, who was working in a school, had found the layout of the building confusing and had got lost during her first day. Another, who worked in a library, did not enjoy the filing in the catalogue; and a third, who had always waited to be told when to go for teabreaks, complained that she had only had two teabreaks during the whole week.

Despite these complaints, for most, if not all, of the pupils the good things about work experience far outweighed the bad. And, in fact, seven said that there were no bad things at all about their experiences. One of them wrote in her log book:

> "This has been the best week out of my school-life. I really enjoyed myself and will miss working in [. . .] when I go back to school. Although the hours were long and my feet got sore I learnt a lot."

Initial fears and subsequent problems

Only one pupil had not been worried about anything before she went out on placement. The rest had, to some extent, been apprehensive yet all but one had found, on the first day, that their fears had been unfounded.

By far the most common fear was about what the people in the workplace would be like, whether they would be friendly and whether the pupils would be able to get on with them.

> "I was frightened in case they weren't very friendly or were grumpy if you didn't pick it up what to do, if they'd moan. I was nervous before I went . . . As soon as the supervisor introduced me to everybody and they were all nice I started to feel okay."

The one boy whose fears and lack of confidence had lasted for more than a day had been frightened to go into the canteen:

". . . in case they all started laughing because they were all talking there and you didn't know what to say. We didna go in to the canteen until the third day. When we went in it was a good laugh. . . . As soon as we went in we found it wasn't as bad as we thought."

Other worries were concerned with going by themselves for the first time into the firm and asking for the supervisor. One of the pupils had taken the easy way out by asking her father to go in with her. The others had simply forced themselves to go in and found that it was much easier than they had anticipated.

Three of the youngsters had been worried about whether they would be able to handle the work and whether they would do something wrong.

"I didna really know much about building sites and didna think I'd get on too well on it. But I got on okay."

There was also general apprehension about what the workplace would be like, how they would get on talking to the public, whether they would get there on time and whether they would get lost in the placement buildings.

When asked whether they had experienced any problems *during* placements, all of the pupils said that they had not.

Direct and incidental learning

We were interested in finding out whether the youngsters had found out anything they had not known before about the workplace or about either themselves or school.

Workplace/working life

Five of the students did not think that they had learned anything about work that they had not known before and another said that the experience had been more or less what he had expected although:

". . . It was easier than I thought it'd be. The way my dad was explaining it, I thought it was real hard work and you had to be really strong [to work in a garage]. But I didn't find it that hard."

In contrast, a boy who had worked in a shop had found it harder then he had expected.

"I was so tired that I just went to bed when I came back home on the first day."

The most frequently mentioned aspect of work that had surprised the students was the wide range of tasks that were involved in particular jobs.

"A sales assistant is a lot harder than the public thinks. There's packing and choosing what to display from the warehouse. They've got a lot of responsibility in thinking what to display and in deciding what will sell. The public just see them as there to help them and there's really a lot more on the other side."

"The thing that struck me most about working in a vet's office was the hours they work. One day you finish at 5.30, but another you could be going until 7.00 if you were busy." (Taken from a log book).

One student had expected the workplace to be "more strict" and was surprised (and pleased) by the relaxed and friendly atmosphere.

Three of the youngsters felt that their placements had enhanced their understanding of society in that they had been given an insight into the adult and working world.

"It gives you . . . an idea of how the real full time workers really work."

Other pupils talked about the skills they had learned (like operating a weighing machine and using a price gun), getting used to working in a big office, getting up early, working longer hours, travelling to work and getting accustomed to "working in the cold".

Themselves

Interestingly, although three of the youngsters felt that they had not learned anything about themselves from work experience and another two were unsure, two-thirds felt that they had improved their understanding of themselves. The most common thing that they had learned about themselves was that they could mix with and get on with adults. They also found out that they were not as shy as they had thought.

"I'm not so shy as I thought I am. Also I learned that I just act the same in school yet they [the workers] treated me as an adult."

"I think you act older when you're with people older than you. I'd never really been just with adults in a place like that before and I found I acted older."

"If you are shy you learn to talk to new people because if you are very shy when you do start work then you may not like your job because you can't talk to anybody because you don't know how."

In addition to acquiring the skills involved in getting to know someone, there was also the important lesson of learning how to cope with people whom you may not like.

"You are in with good and bad company but have to learn to get on with them both."

Another skill that one needed in getting on with people was identified by one boy who found that his experience had helped him to:

". . . be able to talk to a manager and be able to talk to another person if I didn't know what to do."

Other pupils who had been dealing with the public found out that they could do it and that it "wasn't as embarrassing" as they had thought it would be.

Self-reliance had been learned by others:

"It was good experience for me to be able to work without anybody hanging around you . . . The other good thing about it is that I was able to get up without any body coming in to wake me up."

The other main quality that pupils discovered they had was the ability to cope and work hard.

"I learned I was prepared to work hard which isn't always the case in school."

"I found out how far I could stretch myself."

"I learned that I could do more than I thought I could — that I could work things that I never even knew I could do."

School

Pupils were asked two questions about school. Firstly, they were asked if work experience had taught them anything about school that they had not known before and, secondly, whether their experiences had changed the way they felt about school.

Just under half of the pupils said that they had not learned anything about school and that their feelings had not changed. However, among the other pupils, motivating effects were evident.

Four of the youngsters stated that since they had enjoyed their work experience so much they were now more keen to start work than they had been before.

> "You're better off being out at work than being in school. You get to meet other people and it's better than seeing the one person [the teacher] all the time."

> "It was better than school. In school you're sitting writing all the time or doing sums. There [at work] you've a choice, you're not doing pricing for a full day. There are more different things to do."

However, two of these pupils , while keen to get a job, had also come to realise the importance of working hard at school.

> "I canna wait to get a job. I wasna bothered before. But I'm staying on until I'm 18. I'll just get a part-time job or something. Then I'll put in for the polis."

> "I want to get out of school quicker to get a job because I enjoyed it. But I'll have to start working a lot harder [at school] if I want a job."

Three of the youngsters had come to realise, or had had confirmed, the importance of staying on at school. One of these preferred being at school because he had not liked the mechanics of work.

> "I didn't like getting up early and travelling and standing about all day doing nothing. It's better in school."

The other two wanted to continue at school in order to get better qualifications.

> "Although I enjoyed it [work] I decided that there maybe are better jobs if I stayed on for further education and got better qualified."

> "I know how hard it is to get a job and you really have to stick in at school...You've only got the chance once."

One girl, however, was worried about the negative effects of work experience on school aspirations. A friend of hers, after going out on placement, had decided that she wanted to leave school at the end of the year."

> ". . . although she's doing six or seven 'O' levels and could do Highers. But she wants to leave after fourth year to do hairdressing since she did her work experience there. It'd be a complete waste, she's too clever for that. So that's a bad point."

Four other pupils made comments. One girl said that she had learned that school was much harder than work. And another had found that the school's attitude to pupils was different to that common in the workplace.

> "School tends to treat you younger because of the foolish children who get into trouble. They [teachers] are just so used to treating them like that, they just keep it that way."

However, two of the students had had their eyes opened to the value of specific aspects of the curriculum and to the effort put in by teachers.

> "I found that the school helped a lot — the things you'd learned in school. The school helped in a big way to help you figure out what you wanted to do . . . It's made me realise that there is more to school than you think there is. School has learned me about people and what they're like. Before I didn't bother but now I know the teachers better than I did."

> "You don't realise how much the teachers bother until you see something like this. It must have taken [Ms B, the teacher] quite a while to organise and get all the places."

Other experience of work

Other studies have shown that 'work experience already exists for many pupils in a form virtually unrecognised by their schools' (Varlaam, 1983), usually in the form of part-time or summer jobs. It has been found that around half of fifteen-to-sixteen year-olds have such experience, with boys more likely to have than girls. The most common type of job is a paper-round.

This is borne out by our (albeit small) study. Half of the pupils interviewed — five of the seven boys and four of the eleven girls — had had a part-time or summer job. Five of the youngsters (four boys, one girl) had paper-rounds, one worked in a shop on a Saturday and one collected football pool coupons. During the summer holidays, one had worked in a snack-bar and another with his uncle as a carpet fitter.

All of the students felt that their week's work experience had differed qualitatively from their part-time work.

> "It was different. The rules, that kind of thing. I'd met strangers when I was working with my uncle but I didn't

talk to them much. That's why I thought I wouldn't be able to."

"Work experience was a full week, that job [her part-time work] was only on a Saturday. So I didn't find out what it was like during the week. Work experience was different. There were a lot more people there."

Future career intentions

Does work experience influence future job aspirations? If it does, does it do this by changing or reinforcing previous job choices or by opening up new opportunities to those previously undecided?

It turned out among our sample that, after work experience, very few of the pupils had changed their original job intentions. Two were still unsure about what they wanted to do. Of the others, those whose placements were in workplaces which were engaged in the line of work they had originally wanted to do still expressed a desire to find that type of job. Most whose aspirations had differed from the work undertaken at their placements still maintained their original choices. Only four pupils admitted to being directly influenced by their placements in terms of widening the range of jobs they would consider or, conversely, changing their minds. Three mentioned that if they could not get the job of their choice, they would now "consider" finding work that was similar to that which they had experienced on their placements. The fourth student said that before going out on work experience she had been wondering whether to look for work in the retail trade (where her placement was) or hairdressing. After her week's experience she had decided that she would prefer hairdressing although she did say that if she could not obtain that kind of work she "wouldn't mind shop work".

Expectations and experience of work experience

In order to compare the effects which were expected with those that were reported after the week's work experience, we compared a pre-placement written exercise with a post-placement questionnaire. This section looks briefly at the responses of the twenty-one pupils who completed *both* of these tasks. (See Appendix III for a description of the instruments used).

Pupils were most likely to anticipate *and* value in retrospect the outcomes of work experience in terms of providing them with the chance to get used to working so that they would have an idea of what to expect and how to cope when they left school. In

41

particular they saw its value as letting them see what it was like to work with adults, to get up early and work longer hours, and to experience travelling further afield than school.

Gaining relevant experience or obtaining references were the second most frequently mentioned benefits of work experience both before and after placements. It was thought that either written references or the fact that pupils could point out to employers that they had had experience would give them 'the edge' over other applicants.

Other vocational effects were mentioned as being important more often *after* pupils had been out on placement than before. Students valued having learned skills which were different from those come across at school. They also felt that they had been given the opportunity to try out certain jobs in order to see whether they wanted to do this kind of work in the future.

Some of the youngsters mentioned learning life skills (ie finding out how to get on with and deal with other staff, managers and the public) and perceived that they had been placed in more mature roles (ie had been self-reliant, had been treated as an adult). Once again, these effects were more likely to be referred to *after* rather than before placements.

Only a small number of pupils in the post-placement questionnaires gave responses which indicated that they had enhanced their understanding of themselves (eg seeing "how far I can stretch myself", finding out what effects they had on others) or of society (seeing how other people act, their attitudes to their jobs).

So it seems that before placements pupils were likely to think of work experience as preparing them in *general* for the world of work. After having been on their week's placement, students still saw these effects as salient, but their views were enlarged to encompass other more specific vocational and personal effects as well.

4

DISCUSSION

By the time this report is published it will be long out of date for the project. This is simply because as evaluators to the project our first responsibility was to get our findings to inform the Co-ordinator and the Steering Committee while there was time to use them in developing policies and changing strategies, and this we did immediately without waiting for the delay of formal publication. What might be the value of the report beyond this?

The basic rationale for the Castlemilk Project was to provide resources which would allow the schools involved to experiment with ways of improving their practice. But the intention was not to confine the effects to project schools — instead it was hoped that models of practice might materialise which other teachers might find of interest in dealing with similar situations in their own schools. The final section of this report, therefore, explores the lessons which other schools might learn from the Castlemilk experience to improve strategies for fitting work experience into the curriculum.

It is important to realise, of course, that the work experience programme discussed here was not entirely new to the school. Like many aspects of the project, the school chose to build on its existing strengths rather than to start afresh. Enhancements included the extension of the opportunity for work experience to *all* S4 pupils during normal term time; the inclusion of the experience as part of a timetabled 'module' (including briefing and debriefing sessions) and the specific allocation of time for one of the teachers to organise and monitor the scheme including, perhaps most importantly, relationships between the school and the employers. Our report, however, has not focussed solely on these. Work experience is still relatively new in many schools. The study we undertook for the project gave us the opportunity to look at the whole programme and it is this which we discuss here.

First, however, the reader must be alerted to the limitations of our report. This is the case study of a single school which is benefiting from the resources of a specially funded project. It serves a catchment area which is generally recognised to be one of deprivation with disturbingly high levels of unemployment. Furthermore, although part of a large urban area, the range of work experience opportunities within a reasonable distance from the school is limited. Clearly no school is 'typical' but at least the reader should be aware of the way in which this one is particularly atypical. What, given these limitations would we see as being of general interest?

Overview

To begin with, it should be made clear that our data suggest that work experience serves a number of important functions. It is seen by pupils as meeting the traditional aims of such schemes — preparing them for the world of work, providing them with references, allowing them to sample specific jobs and to learn valuable life skills. Second, it appears to have both practical and less tangible benefits for the employers involved. Third, it serves the purpose of breaking down the negative stereotypes that industry sometimes has of certain pupils. Finally, it provides the opportunity to improve understanding and communication between schools and the workplace.

But it is not sufficient to leave work experience vaguely as a 'good thing'. What does this study suggest to be the attributes of the school's approach which made for success? In what ways might it be improved? What aspects of the experience appealed to pupils? Why? What is in it for employers? What is in it for schools? These are all questions we have addressed in the report and which we try to draw together here.

Why did employers consider this work experience scheme a 'success'?

The first clue as to the apparent success of the programme lies in the evidence that employers were impressed by the way in which it had been managed. The school had clearly established a strategy to develop links between the work experience course and employers. The way in which the work experience week was embedded within a structured series of lessons seems to us to be important — even if this did not always work out as intended. That there was a member of staff with clear responsibility both for the course and for liaising with employers strikes us as contributing also to its success. The high level of awareness amongst employers that there was such a link person and her visits or calls while the pupils were on placement perhaps add to our evidence for the importance of such a role. The second likely explanation for the employers' positive reaction stems from the young people themselves. The relative timidity of the youth of 15 is perhaps lost to many of us when met in small groups enjoying themselves in the way adolescents will on Saturday afternoons. But, of course, the vast majority, when on their own, stumbling their way into the adult workplace, are a very different phenomenon. The youngsters had given a good account of themselves. Many of the employers seemed positively to enjoy the opportunity of having these young people working with them.

Of course, as we have made clear, it would be wrong to assume that there is no scope for improvement. In particular we noted that some of the employers wanted more information about where work experience fitted into the curriculum and how it was being followed up after placements. This is a point that should be taken up by schools (and in the case of this school will be in subsequent years). It is important that employers know something about the aims of work experience and how it fits in with the school based 'work' modules. This gives them a better idea of how to organise placement activities in line with the general orientation of the wider 'work' programme and encourages a feeling of greater involvement in the whole scheme. But overall the main reason for the employers' satisfaction with their experience would seem to have been the effort which went into its planning by the school.

How did the young people react?

Although the placements were in a number of different organisations, the one common element was that they were all practically based — the pupils were 'doing' rather than simply observing. This was seen as being of particular importance by the youngsters, as was being engaged in the same work as other staff. In the pupils' own words, they wanted to be "doing real work". The pupils were less satisfied when they were given something different to do from the other workers, when they did jobs that did not require any specific or new skills (eg collecting supermarket trolleys) or when there was nothing to do. So it seems that pupils wanted to make the best of work experience, they wanted to treat it seriously, they wanted to have work to do, they wanted to feel that they had achieved something and they wanted to feel that it had been a 'real' experience of work.

From the point of view of pupil enjoyment, the most important aspect of the placements was not the actual work done, but the relationships they had had with other staff. Worries about other staff and how they might get on with them were the most common causes of apprehension before youngsters went out on placements, but, in practice, almost all of the pupils had got on well with their fellow workers. In addition, most of the students who complained about not doing "real work", or who said that they had not learned anything useful, also mentioned that their contact with other staff had been more limited than it might

45

otherwise have been. So it seems that although vocational elements of work experience are important to pupils, it is the social aspects of work that they enjoy most.

Opinions were divided about the ideal length of placements. While more than half of the employers thought that it should be longer so that pupils had more time to settle in and gain independence, pupils were rather less keen on this extension, principally because they were worried about the time lost from school and the amount of work to catch up on when they returned.

It was clear that, for the majority of young people, this was not seen as a 'training' exercise in the practical skills sense. What they appreciated most was a 'taster' of what it was like to be at work; to experience a work regime; to become part of a team within a workplace. They did not particularly appreciate being given a discrete task to do on their own as this cut them off from the social contact they were looking for.

What are the implications of this? The first is that, if the young people we spoke to are typical (and their arguments were certainly convincing), then this is a message which ought to be conveyed to prospective placement providers. But second, and at a more general level, we wonder whether there is a more basic question about what should be the content of work experience which has yet to be answered. What guidelines should employers be given about their participation? How in fact do they decide what to provide? What is the 'recipe' for maximum benefit both to the young people and to employers involved? We cannot answer these questions from this piece of work but what we observed was that, in trying to answer this, our case-study school seemed to be working in isolation, and this is surely not the best model to adopt.

What's in it for the employers?

We were impressed not only by the reactions of pupils but also by those of the employers. There was a clear willingness to contribute to the success of the venture and, although there had been a few hiccoughs, their commitment appeared to be for the long-term rather than 'one−off'. What lessons might our study therefore have for employers contemplating involvement in such a scheme?

More than half the employers said that they benefited directly in some way from the scheme. This could either be in practical terms (eg an extra pair of hands, a platform for recruitment, good public relations, staff training) or in less tangible forms (eg keeping in touch with the needs and feelings of youngsters, staff seeing their workplace and practices through "new eyes" and increased staff co-operation).

Perhaps in a less obvious way, we, as evaluators discerned influences which we suspect are just as important. Thus, for example, it is interesting that several of the employers assumed that since they had encountered no difficulties with the youngsters that the school must have selected and sent only the 'good' pupils. In fact, as mentioned earlier, all S4 pupils were given the chance to undertake work experience and although it is possible that only the 'good' students took up this opportunity, it seems highly unlikely. A more plausible explanation is that the employers had rather low expectations, either of pupils in general or of youngsters from Castlemilk in particular. It is possible, therefore, that work experience is serving the incidental but — important — purpose of breaking down the negative stereotypes that industry has of young people.

In essence, then, this study suggests that hesitant employers should consider that an *opportunity* may be missed if they decline to involve themselves in such schemes. Perhaps they should be sure that the number of young people they take on at any one time is well within their capacity to keep actively engaged. They should be sure that the young people they receive are well prepared, and indeed one of our recommendations for the case-study school was that they should consider a greater involvement of employers in preparing pupils for work experience. We suspect equally that the attractiveness of such involvement would diminish if it were overused but there was little evidence of this being the case in our study.

What's in it for the pupils?

Pupils and employers had remarkably similar views on the effects of work experience. Both were most likely to see the value of placements in terms of preparing pupils for the world of work (by giving the chance to work with adults, to get up early, to work with the public etc.) and both felt that the experience had vocational potential (eg to see what specific jobs were like and thus reinforce (or change) job choices, and provide pupils with relevant experience (and references) which might improve future job prospects). Much of this type of learning had been expected by the youngsters, but what surprised many pupils was the great variety of tasks and skills involved in particular jobs.

Other more personal effects were also mentioned (though to a lesser extent) both by employers and students. Useful life skills were learned (eg how to talk to other people) and self development, including self-reliance, maturity, and self confidence, was enhanced. Several of the youngsters reported surprise and pleasure at finding out they could get on with people, that they could cope and work hard.

Some pupils mentioned that work experience had changed their attitudes to school. Some were now more keen to leave school, whereas others had realised the value of getting good qualifications and working hard at school. Placements had also had the effect on a few pupils of extending the range of work they would be willing to consider if they could not obtain the jobs of their first choice.

So it seems that work experience is providing for pupils a window on the workplace. Perhaps the window only gives a partial view and perhaps it distorts some aspects of the world of work; but the light shed on events may be qualitatively different from that encountered by the youngsters before.

What's in it for the schools?

Liaison between schools and the workplace is something that many schools are trying to improve. Schools want to improve the knowledge that each has about what the other is trying to do. This study suggests that work experience schemes offer an important opportunity to improve such understanding. Not only do pupils get the chance to see what goes on in the workplace but employers have the opportunity to talk to youngsters while they are still at school and to contribute in a small way to their education. In addition, work experience provides a basis for direct liaison between teachers and industry. Contacts are made during the arrangements for work experience and when teachers visit pupils during placements.

Many of employers in this study valued the opportunity to speak to teachers and to show them something of what was happening in industry. And it is worth noting that about half of the employers said that they were involved in other activities concerned with school/industry liaison —

> "We had groups of youngsters coming out to our store. This gives a wider range of pupils a chance of coming along and just basically telling them about the company, what to expect when they come out to work and really promoting the company in the hope that when they leave school we'll have generated enough interest for them to come along to us to ask for an interview."

> "I've been to schools and talked to groups of leavers. Okay, the teachers tell them more or less about what to expect when they go out to work but they don't always

believe things teachers tell them. But when they're actually speaking to employers, they accept it more from us."

The employers made specific suggestions for ways of linking which might be instigated. Most of these concerned activities similar to those that some of the employers already engaged in: mock interviews; employers, trade unionists and employees going into schools to talk about the kind of work done in their organisations; and groups of pupils visiting different types of workplace.

"They could have people from different walks of life coming in and talking about different things. They could look at the scope of jobs and hear from shop stewards and training officers . . . They [schools] could pick an aspect of work and get someone to talk about it."

Other suggestions included encouraging employers to attend the school's careers evening and teachers going out on placement into industry.

"Teachers should go out into a modern office to keep up to date with the new office equipment. In the school environment you can lose touch with what's happening in the real world, especially in Business Studies. They should know what methods and equipment are now used in an office and how typing practices have changed . . . They could then set up a prototype office that's run like an office and where pupils treat it as an office."

"Guidance teachers could come here and see around the place and find out what shop assistants actually do. They could then go back and set up training facilities in the schools."

Overall, therefore, being a situation where schools and industry are obliged to co-operate, and where also there is evidence that each wants to contribute, it may be that work experience provides an important opportunity for schools to nurture liaison and understanding with industry and break down barriers.

Finally

The burden of our evidence confirms that, at least in our case study, work experience courses are potentially a worthwhile addition to the curriculum. At the same time however, it must be clear from our study that the benefits which might accrue are unlikely to be an *automatic* consequence of a work experience scheme. Those we observed result from this school work experience scheme being one which, although it could be strengthened in a number of ways, is basically a well-constructed and implemented project, owing a lot of its success to the personal commitment of the teacher involved in planning and running it.

With the advent of two-year YTS schemes it may be that work experience as part of the curriculum for 14 to 16 year-olds will diminish in importance if for no other reason than that employers may find that their resources are insufficient to allow them to cope with both. We consider that this would be unfortunate, especially in schools such as the one considered in this report which has established a programme for *all* pupils irrespective of academic attainment and career intentions. The experience of the Castlemilk Project in consciously innovating in this area and in opening their efforts to evaluation would seem to us to have yielded additional evidence that, despite the substantial effort involved both for schools and employers, work experience, as part of the school curriculum, can offer substantial dividends.

References

KERRY, J (1983) 'Work Experience: The Project Trident Approach' *in* Watts A G (ed), *Work Experience and Schools*, London: Heinemann Educational Books.

VARLAAM, C (1983) 'Making Use of Part-time Job Experience' *in* Watts A G (ed), *Work Experience and Schools*, London: Heinemann Educational Books.

WATTS, A G (1983) 'Work Experience: Principles and Practice' *in* Watts A G (ed), *Work Experience and Schools*, London: Heinemann Educational Books.

APPENDIX I: EMPLOYER INTERVIEW SCHEDULE

Name of firm/institution
Name of person in charge of work experience
How long have you been involved in the [case study school] work experience scheme?
Do you offer work experience to pupils from other schools?

---

1) Why did you decide to take part in the work experience scheme?
2) What kinds of activities do the pupils do in your organisation?
3) Do you give pupils any advice about job interviews, recruitment or necessary qualifications for your type of work?
4) Are you able to offer some kind of training or supervision to the pupils? What kind? What does it involve?
5) Have you offered full-time employment or a YTS place to any pupils who have undertaken work experience in your organisation?

The pupils and schools

6) What do you think the pupils gain from work experience?
7) What are your feelings about the amount of time currently available to pupils for work experience?
8) a) What were your general impressions of the pupils who were placed in your organisation?
   b) Are there any particular problems that you have come up against? How might these be overcome?
   c) Was there anything that particularly impressed you about the pupils?
9) What are your feelings about the way that pupils were prepared by the school for work experience?
10) What kind of support have you received from the school? Would you like more or less of this kind of support?
11) Are there any changes that you would like to see in the work experience scheme?

The firms/workplace

12) What are the benefits of work experience for your organisation?
13) What are the benefits of work experience for industry in general?
14) How could links between the schools and the workplace be improved?

APPENDIX II: PUPIL INTERVIEW SCHEDULE

Preparation/Choice/Time

1. I see that you were in . . . for your W.E. placement. Was this your first choice?
   If NO,   What was your first choice?
              Do you know why you were not able to get your first choice?
   If YES, Why did you choose that placement?
2. What do you think about the way that the school prepared you for going out on W.E.?
3. What did you think about the amount of time that you were out on W.E.?

The workplace

4. What sorts of things did you do in . . .? (observation vs. participation)
5. a) Did someone at . . . show you what you had to do?

     b)   Was there someone you could go and ask if you weren't sure what to do?

6. What were the other people like who worked there? How did you get on with them?
7. Did the firm give you any advice about job interviews or about how to get that type of job?
8. Why do you think the firms decided to take part in the W.E. Scheme?

Pupils' perceptions

9. What do you think the purpose of W.E. is?
10. Did you enjoy your W.E.? Why?
11. What were the things you were most worried about before you started your W.E.? Were these things as difficult as you expected?
12. Did you have any problems when you were out on W.E.? What were they and what did you do to try to get over them?
13. (Refer to questionnaire) You said that the good things about working in . . . were . . . Why did you think these things were good?
14. (Refer to questionnaire) You said that the bad things about working in . . . were . . . Why did you think they were bad?
15. (Refer to questionnaire) You said the W.E. might be useful to you in the future because . . . In what way do you think this will help you?
16. a)   Did you learn anything about yourself from W.E.?
     b)   Did you learn anything about what it's like to work?
     c)   Did you learn anything about school from W.E.?
        (What did you learn? Did these things surprise you?)
17. Had you done any other work before you went out on W.E.? For instance, a Saturday job, or a job before or after school.
18. Has W.E. changed or had any effect on the way you feel about school?
19. What would you like to do when you leave school? Has being out on W.E. had any effect on what you want to do? In what way?
20. Are there any changes that you would like to see in the W.E. project?

APPENDIX III: METHODS OF COLLECTING PUPIL DATA

    Data on the pupils' reactions to their work experience placements were gathered in a number of ways. Firstly, it was hoped to gather information on the pupils' expectations from all of the (44) youngsters who were going out in the second block of work experience before they actually took up their placements. English teachers were asked to set these students a writing *exercise* on "How I think work experience will be useful to me". In the event, only 26 pupils completed this task, as one of the teachers was unable to fit this work in.

    Secondly, after the pupils had finished their week's work experience, their teachers once again provided help in distributing and administering a questionnaire which asked the youngsters to write about the good and bad things about being out on placements as well as how they thought the experience might help them in the future. Again, there were difficulties in teachers fitting this task into their schedules and only 33 *questionnaires* were completed.

    Thirdly, 18 of the pupils who had completed the questionnaires were *interviewed* by the researchers in order to question them in more depth about their questionnaire answers, as well as to collect additional information about their perceptions of and reactions to work experience (see Appendix II).

    Finally, the log books which pupils kept during their week's placements and the reports which they subsequently wrote on their experiences were obtained by the researchers and these were used to provide supplementary information.